APPROACH TO DISTANCE

BY THE SAME AUTHOR

POETRY
Overdrawn Account
This Other Life
Entertaining Fates
Lost and Found
About Time Too
Selected Poems
Ghost Characters
The Look of Goodbye
The Returning Sky
Buried Music
Collected Poems 1976-2016

PROSE
Untitled Deeds
Spirits of the Stair: Selected Aphorisms
Foreigners, Drunks and Babies: Eleven Stories
The Draft Will
September in the Rain

TRANSLATIONS
The Great Friend and Other Translated Poems
Selected Poetry and Prose of Vittorio Sereni
The Greener Meadow: Selected Poems of Luciano Erba
Poems by Antonia Pozzi

INTERVIEWS
Talk about Poetry: Conversations on the Art

CRITICISM
In the Circumstances: About Poems and Poets
Poetry, Poets, Readers: Making Things Happen
Twentieth Century Poetry: Selves and Situations
Poetry & Translation: The Art of the Impossible

PETER ROBINSON

APPROACH TO DISTANCE

SELECTED POEMS FROM JAPAN

Translations by Miki Iwata

ピーター　ロビンソン

距離を縮めて　日本からの選詩集

岩田 美喜　訳

ISOBAR PRESS

First published in 2017 by

Isobar Press
Sakura 2–21–23–202, Setagaya-ku,
Tokyo 156-0053, Japan
&
14 Isokon Flats, Lawn Road,
London NW3 2XD, United Kingdom

http://isobarpress.com

ISBN 978-4-907359-18-8

Copyright © Peter Robinson 2017

All rights reserved.

ACKNOWLEDGEMENTS

All the poems translated here are included in Peter Robinson's *Collected Poems* 1976–2016 (Shearsman Books, 2017); many thanks to Tony Frazer at Shearsman for supporting this project. Miki Iwata would like to thank David Money and Andrew Houwen for their invaluable help with the translations. The poem on page 24,「かなしみ」('Distress'), is reprinted by kind permission of the author, Tanikawa Shuntaro. Cover photograph copyright © Diethard Leopold 1994. Author portrait copyright © Jane Dunster 2014.

for Matilde and Giulia

Approach to Distance

Introduction	8
A Dedication	22
Lost Objects	26
The Yellow Tank	30
Leaving Sapporo	34
Deep North	38
After Bansui	42
Aftershocks	50
Italian in Sendai	60
Winter Interiors	62
For My Daughter	64
Coat Hanger	68
Typhoon Weather	72
Animal Sendai	74
Winter Zoo Encounter	78
Equivocal Isle	82
All Around	86
Occasional Sunset	90
Pasta-Making	92
Alien Registration	94
Calm Autumn	96
What Have You	100
From the World	102
Last Resort	106
Silence Revisited	108
All Times Are Local	112

距離を縮めて

はじめに　　　　　　　　　　　9

献辞　　　　　　　　　　　　23

失くしもの　　　　　　　　　27
黄色いタンク　　　　　　　　31
札幌を離れるにあたって　　　35
みちのく　　　　　　　　　　39
晩翠に倣いて　　　　　　　　43
余震　　　　　　　　　　　　51
仙台のイタリア人　　　　　　61
冬の室内　　　　　　　　　　63
娘へ　　　　　　　　　　　　65
ハンガー　　　　　　　　　　69
台風の荒れ模様　　　　　　　73
アニマル・センダイ　　　　　75
冬の動物園での邂逅　　　　　79
あいまいな島　　　　　　　　83
辺り一面に　　　　　　　　　87
たまたまの日没　　　　　　　91
パスタ作り　　　　　　　　　93
外国人登録（エイリアン・レジストレーション）　　　　　　95
静かな秋　　　　　　　　　　97
君が見たものは　　　　　　 101
この世界より　　　　　　　 103
最後の頼りの保養地　　　　 107
再訪の閑さや　　　　　　　 109

あらゆる時間は現地時間　　 113

Introduction

Peter Robinson (1953–) is among Britain's internationally recognized contemporary poets. He has also had a long and deep relationship with Japan. He was born in Salford, Lancashire, raised in Liverpool, studied literature at the universities of York and Cambridge in the 1970s, and began publishing poetry around the same time. After being awarded his doctorate on contemporary poetry from the University of Cambridge in 1981 and teaching for some years in the UK, he came to Japan in 1989, the country where he would spent the next eighteen years. He taught English literature mainly in Sendai and Kyoto, finally leaving the ancient Japanese capital to teach for the Department of English Literature at the University of Reading in 2007. The fourteen years he worked at Tohoku University, Sendai, from 1991–2005 proved an important phase both for his public career and his private life. During this period, he underwent the breakup of his first marriage, endured major surgery to excise a brain tumour, married Ornella Trevisan, from Parma, Italy, and became the father of two daughters. At the same time he published eight volumes of poetry, including his first *Selected Poems*, three monographs of poetry criticism from Oxford University Press, as well as other works of translation and prose. The fact that the first critical collection of writings on his work, *The Salt Companion to Peter Robinson*, edited by Adam Piette and Katy Price, was published in 2007, suggests that his critical acclaim as a poet began to take shape during his Sendai years.

Unsurprisingly, many of the poems written in that period focus on Japan and the people he met there, a selection from which is offered to Japanese readers in this volume. Robinson's poems are almost always concerned with seemingly ordinary occurrences in his life and the lives of those around him, and, to

はじめに

　ピーター・ロビンソン（一九五三―）は、国際的に知られたイギリスの現代詩人の一人であり、また、日本と長く深い関わりを育んでもきた人物でもあります。ランカシャーのソルフォードで生まれ、リヴァプールで育った彼は、一九七〇年代にヨーク大学とケンブリッジ大学で文学を学びましたが、その頃から自分でも詩を発表し始めました。一九八一年に現代詩の研究でケンブリッジ大学から博士号を授与された後は、しばらくイギリス国内で教鞭を執ったのち、一九八九年に日本へやってきました。そこで彼は、二〇〇七年にレディング大学英文学科で教授となるために京都を離れるまでの実に十八年を、主に仙台と京都で英文学を教えて過ごしました。とりわけ、一九九一年から二〇〇五年にわたって仙台の東北大学で教鞭を執っていた十四年間は、彼の仕事にとっても私生活にとっても重要な時期となりました。その間に彼は最初の結婚に終止符を打ち、脳腫瘍の摘出という大手術を受け、パルマ出身のイタリア人オルネラ・トレヴィサンと再婚して、二人の娘の父親となったのです。同時に、彼は最初の『選詩集』を含む詩集を八冊、オックスフォード大学から詩に関する専門研究書を三冊出版し、その他にも翻訳や散文の作品をいくつか著しました。彼についての初めての論文集『ソルト出版社ピーター・ロビンソン必携』（アダム・ピエット、ケイティ・プライス編）が二〇〇七年に出たという事実からも、詩人としてのロビンソンの評価が、彼が仙台にいた時代に高まってきたことが分かるでしょう。

　そんなわけで、この時期に書かれた詩の多くが日本について、そしてそこで彼が出会った人について詠んでいるのも、何ら不思議はないでしょうし、本書が日本の読者に向けて編んだのも、そういった詩作品です。ロビンソンの詩は、ほとんど常に一見何気ない日常の出来事や、彼の身近にいる人々を題材にしており、詩人ウィリアム・ブレイクのことばを借りれば「一握の砂に世界を見る」たぐいのものです。しかし、だからといって彼の詩の世界が狭いとか、彼の伝記に通暁していないと理解できないとかいうことではありません。とはいえ、（この「はじめに」の冒頭で簡単に

borrow a phrase from William Blake, they seek 'To see a world in a grain of sand'. Although it does not follow that the scope of his poetry is small and can only be appreciated by those familiar with his biography, some basic information (such as that outlined in the first paragraph of this introduction) can be a help. Regarding the autobiographical nature of Robinson's poetry, Roy Fisher in his preface to *The Salt Companion* observes that 'the life-images are held separate and inhibited from converging to form a story with a point' so that if we 'push the summary outline of Robinson's life away into another time – any time – and another set of places – any set of places – we can see how transferable its main terms are'. For, beneath the surface of an ordinary life, his poems explore the shared (as well as individual) issues of human existence – the senses of loss, displacement and alienation, memory, the pleasures and pains of love, fleeting moments of epiphany, and much more besides.

'Winter Zoo Encounter', for example, deals on one level with a quite specific day for the poet and his family, when they visited the Yagiyama Zoo, one of their haunts in Sendai. Talking with each other in Italian, they are unexpectedly spoken to by an Italian woman who had married a Japanese man, one assumes, and has lived a long time in the area with her husband's family. She is apparently hungry for any opportunity to speak in her mother tongue and this expresses her sense of isolation. Her loneliness then offers a parallel between herself and the exotic animals in cages removed from their native lands – which finally leads the poet to reflect on his own international marriage and their life in Japan. Here, all is quite concrete and specific. Yet, on another level, this sense of displacement can come to anybody who is away from home, whether domestically or internationally – perhaps even at home as well. After all, you cannot belong to many places at the same time, and when you move from one to another (mentally or physically), you not only have to acclimatize

示した程度の)基本的な情報が役に立つのは間違いありません。ロビンソンの詩が持つ自伝的な要素について、ロイ・フィッシャーは、『ロビンソン必携』の序文で次のように述べています——「生活のイメージは断片的にされたままで、明確な論点を持った物語へと収束しないよう抑制されている」ために、われわれ読者が「ロビンソンの人生のあらましを、別の時代へと——どんな時代でも構わない——そして別の一群の場所へと——どんな場所でも構わない——押しやってしまえば、彼の詩の主要な用語が、いかに置き換え可能かということが分かるだろう」と。なぜなら、日常生活という表向きの背後で、ロビンソンの詩は、人間存在が共有する(また個人で味わうしかない)さまざまな問題を考察しているからです。人間が感じる喪失感、自分の居場所はここではないという気持ち、疎外感、記憶、愛の喜びや痛み、束の間やって来ては去って行く啓示的瞬間など、そういった多くのことが問題になっているのです。

　「冬の動物園での邂逅」を例に考えてみましょう。一面では、これは非常に具体的な、詩人とその家族が仙台でよく訪れていた八木山動物園での、ある一日を詠んだものです。詩人夫婦がイタリア語で話していると、おそらく日本人男性と結婚し、夫の家族とともに長らくこの近所で暮らしていると思われるイタリア人女性から、藪から棒に話しかけられます。その女性は見るからに、母国語で思いの丈を語って自分の孤独感を伝える機会に飢えている感じです。彼女の孤独は、生まれた場所から引き離されて動物園の檻の中にいる異国の動物たちと彼女自身を二重写しにさせます。しかしそれによって詩人自身もまた、自分の国際結婚と、日本での暮らしについて考えざるを得なくなってしまいます。ここまでは、詩が歌う全てはごく具体的で特殊なものです。しかし、別の面から見てみれば、自分がいるべき場所から離れてしまったというこの感覚は、故郷を離れた人であれば(それが国内であろうと国外であろうと)誰にでも訪れうるものでしょう。場合によっては、故郷にいてすら、そういう感覚に襲われることもあります。畢竟、人は一度に色々な場所に属することはできないのであって、ある場所から別の場所へと(精神的にであれ、物理的にであれ)移動をする際には、新しい場所に順応する必要があるだけでなく、もともと自分が属していた古い場所との関係をも再構築しなければならないのです。

yourself to the new place, but also to reconfigure your relationship with the old one to which you originally belonged.

Furthermore, noting that the epigraph attached to this poem is from Randall Jarrell's 'The Woman at the Washington Zoo' (1960), we find a further complexity in Robinson's work. Jarrell's poem reflects on what the woman and the animals in the zoo have in common – 'In the eyes of animals, these beings trapped / As I am trapped but, themselves, the trap'. This is the quotation the poet recalls in 'Winter Zoo Encounter', listening to the stranger's words. However, the ambiguity of the subject in its third verse (in whose mind does the phrase appear?) also allows us to read the citation as if it were her own idea of her current situation, helping transform the American poet's words into a more general voice for people's states of mind.

Thus, the poem covers three different but interrelated layers of experience: first, the real and direct one which the poet encounters; secondly, the general human condition of displacement and alienation; and, finally, the literary experience in which the poet as well as the reader absorb the preceding literary texts so they can contextualize the poem and, accordingly, have a better grasp of what is at issue in it. This contextualizing, which evokes and conjoins historical, cultural, and present experiences of Japan, Italy, America and Britain, as well as of environmental and animal issues suggests how the poem can be understood to work against the separations it evokes and encounters.

Intertextual relations thus play a large part in Robinson's poems. Merely browsing the pages of this volume, you will notice that many of them have epigraphs – lines both widely known and, sometimes, obscurely personal. A good example of the latter is 'Alien Registration', which adopts a slip of the tongue by the then assistant from the English Department at Tohoku University. Instead of 'alien registration card', she mistakenly advised the poet to renew his 'alienation card'. This produced a

それに加えて、この詩に添えられた題辞——ランドル・ジャレルの「ワシントン動物園の女」（一九六〇）からの引用——に注目すれば、ロビンソンの作品にはさらに複雑な位相が存在することが分かります。ジャレルの詩は、動物園にいる女と動物達に共通しているものは何かを思案して、「動物たちの目の中、彼らも囚われの身だけど／囚われの私みたいに、自分が檻なわけじゃない」と謳います。この詩行は、「冬の動物園での邂逅」では、詩人がくだんの女性の話を聞きながら思い出す一節になっています。しかし、第三連の主語の曖昧さ（一体この一節は、誰の心にふと思い浮かんだのでしょう？）が、これはその女性が自分の状況について自分でふと思いついたことばではないかという読み方をする余地をも、読者に与えています。それによって、アメリカの詩人のことばが、もっと普遍的な人間の心の声へと変換されるのです。こうしてこの詩は、三層の異なる、しかし互いに関連した経験を同時に提示しています。まず基層には、詩人が遭遇した現実の直接的な経験があります。しかしその次には、自分が属していない場所にいるという感覚や疎外感という人間の普遍的な条件があります。そして最後に、詩人と読者がともに、先行する文学テクストを吸収することで、この詩が問題にしていることをより深く把握するという文学的な経験が来るのです。このように、日本、イタリア、アメリカ、イギリスにおける、環境や動物の問題をも含めた、歴史的、文化的、そして今ここの経験を、この作品が文脈の中で考えていることは、この詩が喚起し、遭遇する〈分け隔て〉というものに、実は対抗する働きかけをしていると考えられるのです。

　かくして、ロビンソンの詩においては、間テクスト的関係性が重要な役割を果たしていることが分かります。本詩集をぱらぱらとめくってみるだけでも、読者は多くの詩に題辞が付されていることに気づくでしょう。それは、よく知られた文章のこともあれば、一般には知られていない個人的なもののこともあります。後者の好例として、「外国人登録」の題辞が挙げられますが、これは東北大学英文学科の当時の助手による言い間違いを表しています。「外国人登録カード（エイリアン・レジストレーション）」と言うべきところ、くだんの助手は間違えて詩人に「疎外感カード（エイリアネーション）」を更新するように告げてしまったというわけです。これが面白いきっかけとなって登録証更新に関わる

humorous opportunity for a poem which conveys the poet's unhappy memory of such bureaucratic chores, coupled with the gloomy weather (the combination of the two forcibly making him conscious of how strange he is to Japanese society even after spending such a long time here). In other poems such as 'Lost Objects', the intertextuality is indirect and less visible. Describing the Japanese custom of placing a lost object in full view, the poet personifies lost objects and, in turn, objectifies himself as a kind of lost property in a strange country. Behind this reversal lies a poem by Shuntaro Tanikawa called 'Distress' ('Kanashimi'), in which the narrator is 'at the transparent past's station / standing in front of its Lost & Found', unable to find 'something horribly important' that he has lost. The point here is that, while Tanikawa focuses on time, or the irrevocability of the past, Robinson adds the problem of out-of-place-ness to his source text. Being out of place is the destiny of lost property by definition, but it is especially so for foreigners in Japan, where they may sometimes feel like a blue purse placed on a fire escape.

'Pasta-Making' is a paean to the poet's Italian wife, which consists of one long sentence stretching across twenty-two lines (a sentence that doesn't end even at the end of the poem). As well as imitating a piece of spaghetti, this also forms a reassuring sense of continuity in their everyday life. Similarly, 'For My Daughter' loosely follows the tradition of poets speaking to their infants. However, while preceding poems such as S. T. Coleridge's 'Frost at Midnight' (1798) and W. B. Yeats's 'A Prayer for My Daughter' (1919) characteristically incorporate a casual, conversational style into contemplations of larger issues relating to nature, morality, or nation, Robinson's version sticks to the world as his little daughter sees and understands it. Thus, the poem ends with a prayer for her healthy laughter 'at these ordinary arrangements of things'. Her name, Matilde, is echoed in the epigraph as 'Miss Matty', but the fact that this is from Elizabeth Gaskell's *Cranford* (1853), in

官僚的な事務作業のつらさと、悪天候が組み合わさった嫌な思い出についての詩が生まれたのでした（この組み合わせは、これほど長い時間を日本で過ごしてきたのに、それでも自分は日本社会にとって〈ガイジン＝よそ者〉だということを、否が応でも詩人に思い出させたのです）。「失くしもの」のような他の詩では、間テクスト性はこれほど直接的ではなく、分かりにくくなっています。誰かが失くしたものを発見した人が、それを見えやすいところに置いておくという日本の慣習を描写しつつ、この作品で詩人は失くしものを擬人化すると同時に、逆に自分のことを、知らない国で落とされた一種の失くしものとして擬物化しています。この逆転の発想の裏にあるのは、谷川俊太郎の「かなしみ」という詩で、この詩の語り手は、「何かとんでもないおとし物を／僕はしてきてしまったらしい」ということに気がついて、「透明な過去の駅で／遺失物係」の前に立ち尽くしています。ここで大事なのは、谷川が主題を時間――過去は取り戻せないということ――に絞っているのに対し、ロビンソンは材源のテクストに〈場違い感〉の問題を加えていることです。場違いなところに存在するというのは、定義の上からも失くしものの宿命であるわけですが、時に自分がまるで「非常階段の上」に置かれた青い財布のように感じる在日外国人にとっては、これは特に切実な問題なのです。

　「パスタ作り」は、詩人のイタリア人の妻に対する賛歌で、二二行の全てが長い一文から成っています（しかも文法的には、詩が終わっても文は完結しません）。これは長細いスパゲッティの形状を模していると同時に、夫婦の日常生活が連綿と続いていくのだという安心感を醸し出しています。同様に家族を詠んだ「娘へ」は、詩人が自分の幼子に歌い掛けるという英詩の伝統をゆるやかに継承しています。しかし、S・T・コールリッジの「真夜中の霜」（一七九八）や、W・B・イェイツの「娘への祈り」（一九一九）といった先行作品が、くだけた会話体を用いながら、それが自然や道徳、国家といった大きな問題への瞑想に結びついていくという特徴を持っているのに対し、ロビンソンの場合は、幼い娘が見て理解している世界から離れようとはしません。こうして、「娘へ」は、「こういう平凡な出来事」に対する娘の健康な笑いを言祝ぐ祈りで終わっています。娘の名前である「マティルダ」は、題辞に

which Miss Matty is described as a kind-hearted, but practically helpless old miss, offers another humorously fond twist to these 'arrangements of things'. Readers may explore here not only the subtle shadows of isolation and alienation in human life, but also a great many small, yet significant, joys in reading these poems.

Among the poems included in the volume, 'All Times Are Local' is unique in that it was written after the poet's return to the UK, but it is also a companion piece to the aforementioned 'For My Daughter'. In 'All Times Are Local', Robinson writes about his younger daughter, Giulia, who seems to be struggling to integrate her former life in Japan with her current one. She is, so to speak, living in two different times at the same time. However, this does not imply a simple binary opposition of past and present. As the title clearly shows, the time she spent in Japan is imagined as a kind of time difference, which implies that both times are in fact present. Of course, the situation is not confined to the younger daughter but true of the whole family, yet with necessary differences among each member, which is subtly reflected in the reference to Ludwig Wittgenstein's idea of 'family resemblance' in the third stanza. Thus, the poem as an epilogue can justify the whole volume, suggesting that Robinson's interest in Japan remains a matter of 'here and now' rather than being a gathering of old memories.

Finally, I would like to add a few words about the present volume and my translations. The book contains poems composed during Robinson's years in Japan (except 'All Times Are Local', as explained above) and arranged in approximately chronological order. Since it is quite impossible to convey both the form and the content of the original in my Japanese versions, I have concentrated on communicating their meaning, at inevitable cost to the transmission of metre, rhythm, rhyme, and cadence. I have, though, endeavoured as far as possible to represent these indispensable elements of poetry, but I should say with regret that much

記された「ミス・マティ」にこだましています。ところが、これはエリザベス・ギャスケルの『クランフォード』から取られており、作中のミス・マティが優しいけれども実務はからきし駄目な年老いた独身女性であるという事実は、「平凡な出来事」にさらなる剽軽で心あたたまるひねりを加えているのです。読者はこうした詩を読みながら、人生にまつわる孤独や疎外感の陰を見出すかもしれません。しかしそれだけではなく、多くのささやかな、けれども大事な、喜びをも見出すことができることでしょう。

「あらゆる時間は現地時間」は、本書に収められた作品の中でも、詩人がイギリスへ帰国した後に書かれたという点では特殊な位置を占めますが、先に述べた「娘へ」と対になる詩でもあります。「あらゆる時間は現地時間」では、ロビンソンは下の娘のジュリアについて歌っているのですが、彼女はかつての日本での暮らしと今の暮らしをうまく統合できずに、苦しんでいるようです。いわば彼女は、二つの異なる時間を同時に生きているのです。しかし、だからといって単なる「過去と現在」の二分法がここでほのめかされている訳ではありません。詩のタイトルからもはっきりと分かるように、日本で暮らした時間は一種の〈時差〉だと想像されており、それは取りも直さず両方の時間が現在だと示唆されているということです。もちろん、状況は娘ひとりに限ったことではなく、家族全体に当てはまることですが、それでも家族の一人一人にそれ相応の必然的な違いは出てくるでしょう。こうした感覚は、第三連のルートヴィッヒ・ウィトゲンシュタインによる「家族的類似」という概念への言及のうちに、巧妙に反映されています。かくして、この詩は本書全体のエピローグとして、その意義をよく示していると言えましょう。ロビンソンが日本に寄せる関心は、単なる思い出の集積などではなく、〈今、ここ〉の問題であり続けているのです。

最後に、本書とその翻訳について、少しばかり付言したいと思います。本書は、(上述のように「あらゆる時間は現地時間」を例外として)ロビンソンが日本にいた時期に書かれた詩を、おおよそ時系列に沿って収録したものです。原文の形式と内容を、拙訳の日本語とともに伝えることは不可能ですので、拙訳では内容(意味)を伝えることに重点を置きました。そのため必然的に、英語の韻律やリズム、脚韻や抑揚などの伝達を犠牲にしています。もちろん、こうした詩に欠くべからざる要素を能う限り

has been lost in translation. Especially when there is word play in English, my Japanese translations tend to lack its brevity – the soul of wit – since I have tried to convey both meanings in the joke. Japanese readers are ardently recommended to read the originals aloud, after getting the sense from the translation. To Peter Robinson, in his seminars and tutorials during my years as a graduate student, I owe much of my appreciation of lyric poetry in English, and if my experience is anything to go by, I am sure you will find a great deal of pleasure in reading these poems, especially out loud, or listening to them being read.

Miki Iwata

日本語で伝えるように努力はしたのですが、残念ながら翻訳で失われたものは多いと白状せざるをえません。特に、英語でことば遊びがある場合、日本語の拙訳では、かけてある二つの意味を両方とも訳出しようとしたために、知恵の精髄と言われる[『ハムレット』の大臣ポローニアスがそう言っています]簡潔さが、少なからず消えてしまいました。日本の読者の皆さんは、訳文で意味をつかんだ後は、ぜひ原文を音読してみてください。わたし自身が英語で書かれた叙情詩の鑑賞能力を育てるにあたっては、大学院生時代に受けたピーター・ロビンソンのゼミや個人指導がとても大きな意味を持っていました。もしも、わたしの経験になにがしかの意味があるのなら、皆さんもこれらの詩を、朗読したり、人が朗読するのを聴いたりすることで、大きな喜びを得られるだろうと、信じています。

岩田美喜

Approach to Distance

距離を縮めて

A DEDICATION

In this quiet district, Shugakuin,
that rustling by the kitchen was
a tomcat I'd been warned of at my rubbish?

No, a large black crow with mocking caw
flaps to my neighbour's roofline
undaunted as I'm opening the back door.

Not samurai helmets in a river park, no,
they're firemen's and, from Kitayamadori, fireflies
darting on the hillside are headlamps of cars.

So I approach to distance, as you hear,
in the telephone's echo and delay.
Misunderstandings overlap, blur; things interfere.

O far interlocutor of my partial care,
for the long moments into silence now I say
words of explanation and launch them on the air.

献辞

修学院、この静かな界隈で
台所でかさこそ音が立ったのは
警告を受けた雄猫が、ぼくのゴミを漁っていたのだろうか。

違う。大きな黒いからすが、人をばかにしたかーという鳴き声で
ご近所さんの屋根並みへぱたぱた飛んで行く、
ぼくが裏口を開けても怯むことなしに。

違う。河岸公園に見えるのは武将の兜、じゃない、
消防士のヘルメットだし、北山通から丘の方へ
突進してゆく蛍は、車のヘッドライトだ。

そんな風に、ぼくは距離を縮めるほどに遠ざかる、電話の声が
こだまして、遅れて届くのを、君が聴いている間にも。
互いの誤解がかち合ってぼやける。互いの事情が邪魔をする。

おお　ぼくがとりわけ気にかける(でも常にではない)、遠くの対話者よ
沈黙へと変わってゆくその長い間に、今ぼくは
説明の言葉をつむぎ、それを電波に乗せて空へと飛ばす。

あの青い空の波の音が聞こえるあたりに
何かとんでもないおとし物を
僕はしてきてしまったらしい

透明な過去の駅で
遺失物係の前に立ったら
僕は余計に悲しくなってしまった

谷川俊太郎「かなしみ」

Here where the sound of that blue-sky wave's heard
it feels as if I've lost
something horribly important

At the transparent past's station
standing in front of its Lost & Found
I've become yet more distressed

Tanikawa Shuntaro, 'Distress'

LOST OBJECTS

A blue purse on a fire-escape!
In this country it's a custom.
Finding some lost property,
a ring, or this blue purse here,
considerately someone
will place it in full view nearby
on a wall, a window sill.

Everywhere you notice them
precariously balanced
on arm-rests of commuter trains
or a bridge's curving parapet,
some person's pocket book, a diary
– these mementos patiently
awaiting whose return?

Seen from tiered expressway lanes
or the Shinkansen tracks,
misplaced items interrupt skylines.
It's Liberty with her torch upraised,
a Bavarian castle: love hotels
are something missing floated clear
of flats and close-packed houses.

As the rush-hour services clatter
through residential districts
on balconies washed sheets flutter,
whole conurbations of them;
in entryways, a clutter
of bikes, umbrellas, shoes has found
some means of coming home.

失くしもの

なんとまあ、非常階段に青い財布が。
この国ではこれが習慣なのだ。
指輪だとか、この青い財布とか
誰かの落とし物を見つけると、
思いやりから、誰かがそれを
近くのよく見える場所においてくれる。
塀際や、窓枠なんかに。

そこら中、そういう失くし物だらけだ。
通勤列車の座席の肘掛けや
橋の丸い欄干の上に
ちょっと危ういバランスで乗っかっている
誰かさんの札入れや手帳
——こういった思い出の品々は、誰のところへ
帰る日を待っているのだろうか。

高架橋の高速道路や
新幹線の線路から外を眺めていると、
場違いなものが色々と地平線上で目立って見える。
松明を手に掲げた自由の女神や
バイエルン風のお城。ラブ・ホテルは
アパートや立て込んだ住宅街の中で
くっきりぽかんと浮かんだ失くし物。

ラッシュ・アワーの電車が
住宅街をガタゴトと通り抜けると、
ベランダに干されたシーツがはためく、
洗濯済みのシーツが織りなす大都会。
マンションの入り口にある、ごちゃごちゃした
自転車や、傘や、靴は、家に戻る
何らかの手段を見つけたのだ。

Leaving a local station platform
under white sky filled with heat,
a memory, loved one, or poem
has been left behind. But what?
Wordless in front of the next
lost property office's window
you find yourself looking perplexed.

熱気のこもる白い空の下
ローカル線の駅のプラットフォームを後にすると、
ひとひらの記憶、愛しい人、あるいは詩を
置いてきてしまったことに気付く。でも何を？
隣にある遺失物拾得所の
窓の前に言葉もなく立てば
そこに映る自分は途方に暮れた顔。

THE YELLOW TANK

for Diethard and Waltraud Leopold

Only a yellow water tank
stained with rain smears and some rust
on a flat apartment roof –
it stares at you from room to room;
and far too near to have perspective,
you could think this yellow tank
a punch in the eye or personal affront
as it shifts above the breakfast table.

Glimpsed through dwarf palm fingers
on your balcony, the thing can seem
a beach resort accessory
or ready-made in an art museum:
its service ladder and overflow
have elegant hooks like croziers,
raised rabbits to imply a joke,
philosophers' scare-marks or sows' ears.

Not funny, a memory of sunlight
throughout the rainy season,
it penetrates our mist-filled mornings,
reconciles three elements.
I've seen it graced by cloudless nights,
full moons, and briefly perching crows;
against the hillside's heaving pines
the yellow tank is all repose.

黄色いタンク

  ディータート・レオポルトとヴァルトラウト・レオポルトに捧ぐ

ただの黄色い貯水タンクだ、
雨だれやさびで汚れて
アパートの屋上にあるのは——
こいつは屋上から部屋の中をじっと見つめる。
あまり近くにあるもので遠近の感覚が失われ、
この黄色いタンクが、たまたま朝食のテーブルの上に位置すると、
まるで目の玉にパンチを食らったか
故意に侮辱されたみたいな気分になる。

ベランダのテーブル椰子の葉越しに
ちらりと見やれば、タンクは
ビーチ・リゾートの飾り物か
美術館の「レディ・メイド」に見えなくもない。
タンクの業務用梯子と配水管には
司教杖みたいな素敵な鉤が付いているけど、
冗談を意味する跳ね兎や、
哲学者が疑問に思った語句に付す引用符、あるいは豚の耳にも
  見える。

まじめな話、梅雨時に太陽の光のことなど
なつかしく思い出していると、
タンクは霧の立ちこめた朝、そこにしっとりと溶け込んで、
自然の三要素を和解させてくれる。
タンクは、雲一つない夜、満月の晩、または
つかのま留まった烏に、趣を添えられていたこともある。
岡の斜面の風に揺れる松林に対し、
黄色いタンクはどっしりと安らいでいる。

Rather than melting snowy ranges,
nippled hills, golf nets, roof-tiles,
afforestation, or glimpse of ocean,
maybe you prefer this tank;
as with a disaffected child,
photograph, make fusses of it,
until the yellow water tank blesses,
answers us back with words.

ひょっとしたら、雪解けの山並みに
隆起した丘、ゴルフ・ネットや瓦屋根、
林野や、海が垣間見える風景、
そんなものよりこのタンクの方が好ましいかもしれない。
駄々っ子と一緒にいるときのように、
写真を撮って、ちやほやしてみるんだ、
ついには黄色い貯水タンクもそれを讃えて、
言葉でもって答えるようになるまで。

LEAVING SAPPORO

for Teruhiko Nagao

This had not happened before.
You'd stopped your car askew outside the airport.
Running to the check-in desk I caught
a girl's polite-voiced information:
'I'm sorry; I'm afraid, sir, this flight has gone.'
And turning, at a loss, I saw
the tail-plane taxi from its boarding gate.

Then the feeling of falling back into a place
with labels, lounges, luggage carousels
had baffled and arrested me,
the projects, a whole day's purpose dissipating
to a huddle of executives wreathed in smoke.
Outbound flight-lists; merely waiting,
I was too disaffected to view the famous lake,
as if life itself had gone on stand-by
and there'd be no escape to make.

But all morning you were standing by.
Daylight thickened on the café windowpane.
A sheaf of tickets in my hand, I'd try
this or that flight, destination or airline,
anything, it seemed, to get into the sky
and, failing, noticed *Welcome to Hokkaido*
once again; and when we met again
you'd be working on your sense of shame.
Although I said it didn't much matter
whether I reached home sooner or later
you said you'd always hold yourself to blame.

札幌を離れるにあたって

長尾輝彦氏に捧ぐ

こんなことは初めてだ。
きみは空港の外で、斜めのまま車を停めた。
チェックイン・カウンターへと走るぼくの耳に
女性の丁寧な声で、お知らせが聞こえた。
「申し訳ございません。お客様、この便は出発済みでございます。」
途方に暮れて振り向くと、
水平尾翼が搭乗口から離れ、滑走してゆくのが見えた。

すると、荷札やラウンジや荷物運搬コンベアのある場所に
無理やり引き戻されたような気持ちが、
ぼくを困惑させ、しっかり捕まえてしまった。
今後の予定やその日の目的が全て、ビジネスマンの
一団がくゆらす煙の中へと雲散霧消したのだ。
出発便の一覧。ひたすらの待ちぼうけで、
あまりに不満な気持ちが溜まり、かの有名な湖など見る気にも
　　なれない。
まるで人生そのものがキャンセル待ちになってしまい
何処にも逃げ場がないかのようだ。

けれどきみは午前中ずっと傍らに待っていてくれた。
カフェの窓に差す日光が強くなった。
チケットの束を手に、ぼくはあの便この便
あの到着地、この航空会社と、
空へと離陸しそうなものなら何でも試したが、
上手くいかずに、ふと気付けばまた
「北海道へようこそ」の看板。ぼくらがまた会ったとき、
あなたは自責の念に駆られていたのだろう。
大したことはないですよ、遅かれ早かれ
家には帰れるのだから、とぼくが言っても
あなたは、今後いつでも自分は責任を感じるだろうと言った。

Blame the unfinished expressway spur,
polythene flounces on its elevated sections,
the sculpture of its stanchions petrified from cloud;
or blame that Monday morning traffic
with queues as when a lorry's shed its load;
blame a continuous drizzling rain
which taunted squeaky windscreen wipers
down an approach road's outer lane;
blame the unforeseen through which we live,
this intimate running up against a sullen sky
and chance encounter with a city fringe's detail
– but, yourself, forgive.

責めるなら、工事中の高速道路の支線だ、
その高架区画に被さっていたポリエチレンのひだ飾り、
雲が石化したかのような柱だよ。
責めるなら、あの月曜の朝の渋滞、
トラックが積み荷を点々とこぼしたかのような長蛇の列。
責めるなら、進入路の外側車線を降りたときに
きいきいと鳴る車のワイパーをからかうようだった、
あのこやみなく続いた霧雨。
責めるなら、ぼくらが生きている世界の予測不能なもの全て、
どんよりした空にどんどん近づいたこと、
街のはずれで起こった数々の瑣末なことがら、
——でも、自分のことは、許してあげなくては。

DEEP NORTH

'What silence
penetrating rock
the voice of the cicada'
Matsuo Bashō

On the platform at Sendai
waiting brought up this example:
were there one or more voices
in his cicada verses,
silence penetrating rock
at a local mountain temple?
'They're plural,' you'd reply.

And were close readers
of the English graveyard school
code-breakers redeployed
once hostilities had ended?
I wondered was it true,
your half-serious theory
that Bashō was a government spy?

Wood stakes at Yamadera
were memorials for their dead
with new names to fend off terror
at death, you might have said
staring at rice fields and roof-shapes
from the highest viewing platform –
inspiration for a visiting poet.

みちのく

「閑さや
　岩にしみいる
　蝉の声」
　松尾芭蕉

仙台駅のホームで待っている間に
こんな訳例ができてしまった。
蝉の俳句の「声」というのは
単数かな、複数かな？
静寂が岩を貫く
地方の山寺のあれだ。
「複数形だね」と、きみは答えることだろう。

それから、英国の墓場派を
精読した者たちは、
戦争が終わって道を変えた
暗号解読者だったんだろうか？
あれは本当だったのかなあ、
松尾芭蕉が政府のスパイだったっていう、
きみの半分本気の持論は。

山寺にある板杭の数々は
死者のための卒塔婆だよ、
臨終の恐怖を寄せつけないために
戒名をつけてあるんだ、って
きみは確か、田圃と屋根並みを
展望台から見つめながら、言ったような──
探訪の詩人が霊感を得るようにと。

But I would be obliged to wait,
let sound sink into stone.
A noise of gunfire, I supposed,
uncovered thoughts of someone
dead ten years, but no less hurt
at warfare and war's echoes.
It was just a bird-scarer's report.

でも、ぼくは待たなくてはならないだろう、
音が石にしみいるがままに任せて。
銃声が、十年前に死んだ誰かの、
今なお戦争と戦争のこだまで
傷つく思いを
露わにしたように思った。
それは鳥威しの音に過ぎなかったのだけれど。

AFTER BANSUI

'And maps can really point to places
Where life is evil now:
Nanking ...'
W. H. Auden

I

Steps climbed into bushes
at a turning as the road
chicaned through curtain walls;
a sign's arm pointed at rushes.

By hinge-posts, leaves and berries
papered over faults where blossom
of late-flowering cherries
had stained grey pavement.

Further, a pine-coned path
snaked by grazed bark, the shins
of pines, and headlight shards
glinted over reddened earth.

These fragments of a car
or scooter come to grief
were more *memento mori*
of each bright thing's brief life.

That evening, walking home
across the castle site, I saw
grass stalks pierce crazed asphalt
like so many flashing swords,

晩翠に倣いて

「そして地図は今や生きることが悪となっている地を
本当にはっきりと示し得るのだ、
南京……」
W. H. オーデン

　　　　　一

石段は藪へと入っていった、
カーテンのひだ折みたいな石垣に消えてゆく
道の曲がり角で。
看板の矢印は、藺草の茂みを指すばかり。

蝶番のついた柱の傍で、木の葉や小さな果実が
断層を包み込んでいたが、
そこでは遅咲きの桜の実が
灰色の敷石にしみを作っていた。

さらに行けば、松ぼっくりだらけの道が
削れた樹皮や、松のむこうずねや、
赤っぽい土の上にちらちら光るヘッドライトの鱗型
のせいで、蛇のように曲がりくねっていた。

事故を起こした車や
スクーターの欠片は
さらなる〈死を想え〉のしるしだった、
あらゆるきらびやかなものの生命の儚さを伝えて。

その晩、城址を通り抜けて
帰宅する途中に、ぼくが見たのは
ひび割れたアスファルトを貫いて生える草の茎が
たくさんの煌めく剣のようなさま、

a full moon scud through trees
above these green remains
of fortifications, its pale face
as in the local poet's lines.

   2

A traffic-filled street in the city bears his name,
its glittering offices clearly seen
beyond this castle's fire-bombed gatehouse,
from an approach road cresting the rise
as it twists through outworks of a wooded mound.

Here was the place by which he'd mourned
changes under a vine-strewn wall.
The moon above that ruined castle
shone an unchanged, luminous glow
while for centuries the structure stood its ground.

So where is the brilliance of long ago?
No ghostly retainer or GI Joe
is transferred over white cars and coaches
convoying tourists by the switchback road
you climbed, fumes fog-like in those pines
where the occupying armies once camped round.

   3

Now when the emperor was restored
these trees were on the losing side:
their trunks, paralyzed sentries;
leaves, plumes shaking in a breeze.

満月が樹々の間、この青々と茂った石垣の
残骸の上を疾走するさま、
月の青白い顔は
ちょうど郷土の詩人の歌のよう。

　　　　二

市街の交通量の多い通りには彼の名前がついている、
その通りのぎらぎら光るオフィス・ビルが
空襲に遭った城の大手門跡からでもはっきり見える、
登城口から、上り坂がてっぺんに至る
板張りの塁をめぐらせた外堡の間をくねくねと縫って。

ここがその場所。詩人が蔦の絡まる
城壁の下で、世の無常を嘆いたという。
あの荒城にかかる月が
変わらぬ、皓々とした光を放った。
何世紀もの間この建造物は持ちこたえて来たというのに。

昔の光今いずこ？
亡霊と成り果てた領主の姿も、進駐軍の米兵も、
白い車やバスで運ばれて来はしないのだ。
徒歩客が登ってきた切り返し道路のすぐそばで観光客を
運ぶ車の、その白煙が松林にかかる霧のよう——
かつて占領軍が駐留したこの松林。

　　　　三

さて、王政復古の大号令の際には
この松林は敗残者の側だった。
数々の幹は、麻痺して動けない歩哨たち。
葉は、微風にそよぐ兜の羽根飾り。

Holding the hill gave material advantage.
Power gravitated in an earlier age
to this natural fortress of river cliffs and gorges.
Partly dismantled by restoration forces,
the rest burnt down in a single bombing raid.
Inside its main defensive walls
a statue of the warlord on his horse
with one blind eye and helmet's crescent moon
overlooks the city's blinking neon.
Here his past reappears in simulation –
come back as a wheeling bird's-eye-view
of lookout towers, the banquet halls,
and peacock-painted sliding screens
are reconstructed as computer graphics
on a series of flickering video screens.

    4

From a plinth in ornamental shrubbery
this dress-coated, bronze politician
has blank eyes fixed on an era of wars:
his selectively related histories
miss live experiments, rapes,
when just remembered foreigners died
(however much it's denied, denied
by interested voices) and maps
could really point to places
where life was evil then, perhaps.

山を手中に収めれば、かなりの優位が得られた。
昔の時代は権力者が惹きつけられたのだ、
河崖と峡谷に挟まれたこの自然の要塞に。
一部は維新政府軍に破壊され、
残りは一夜の大空襲で焼き払われた。
その中核的な防御壁、本丸の中には
藩主の騎馬像が
その独眼と三日月の前立の兜でもって
市街のまばゆいネオンを見下ろしている。
ここでは、彼の過去がシミュレーションで再現され——
回帰するのだ、物見の塔から見た
回転式の鳥瞰図、大広間、そして
孔雀が描かれた襖などが
何度も明滅を繰り返すビデオのスクリーンに
CGで現れると。

   四

装飾的な植え込みに埋もれた台座から
この燕尾服の、ブロンズ像の政治家が
空虚な瞳で戦争の時代をじっと見ている。
選択的に語られる彼の歴史には
人体実験もレイプも出て来はしないが、
その時実は、かろうじて記憶されるだけの外国人たちが死んだし、
(どれほど否定されようと、利害関係者の
声に否定されようと)そして地図は
そのとき生きていたことが悪だった地を
本当に示し得た——のかもしれない。

5

Bansui, you're their local poet not mine.
With your moon-viewing parties and blossom
of the late-flowered cherry, a pink stain
on grey pavement, glimpsed against the hum

coming through trees from a tour bus engine,
a uniformed girl at its door waves her pennant
beckoning veterans or children by the shrine
to their war dead: that's what blossom meant;

and though some still insist it never was,
others have been ready to apologize at last
for the mounds of unearthed skulls, the burden

of documents in archives, stored or lost,
that would likely vindicate the poet Auden
in his journeying to and from those wars.

五

晩翠、あなたは彼らの郷土の詩人であって、ぼくのではない
月見の宴や、あの遅咲きの桜、
灰色の敷石の上の桃色のしみが、
かすかなブンブンいう音に対峙するようにちらりと見える

が、それはツアー・バスのエンジン音が樹々の向こうから聞こえて
　　くるのだ。
バスの扉口では制服を着た女性が旗を振って
神社のそばにたむろする老人や子供を手招きしている、
死者の元へ。それがはかない桜花の意味するところ。

未だにそんなことは起こらなかったと主張する人もいるけれど
もう謝罪する用意ができている人もいる
発掘された山のような頭骨に対し、公文書館にあった、

現存あるいは遺失した大量の文書に対して──
それらはおそらく、詩人オーデンと
彼が戦争を行き来した旅の擁護になるだろう。

AFTERSHOCKS

1

That year, college started late;
pigeons fed on uncut lawn
about a reminiscent court,
its peonies in full bloom.

Mock frontages, a cross
between Italian seminary
and New England campus,
sported scaffolding, debris –
silence by each damaged classroom.

2

There were crazes in façades
of burnt ochre, sienna roof-tiles
hung with wisteria flowers
like Parma violet waterfalls
and the small, untended shrine
had staggered like a salary-man,
pine pillars lifted off their stone
bases, all its saké downed.

3

From music school windows
came phrases, tricky scales
on disparate pianos
practising western intervals.

余震

　　　　一

その年、大学は遅れて始まった。
鳩がぼうぼうに伸びた芝生の上で餌をついばんでいた
記念公園の辺りだ、
芍薬が満開だった。

古典建築の正面を模した建物、イタリア式神学校と
ニュー・イングランドの大学キャンパスの
合の子みたいな何か、
飾りのように組まれた足場、瓦礫――
壊れた教室から漂う静寂。

　　　　二

黄土と赤土でできた瓦屋根の
ファサードにはひびが入っていた、
そこには藤の花がさがっていて
ニオイスミレでできた滝のよう、
小さな、手入れの行き届いていない神社が
ぐらついていた様子はサラリーマンのよう、
松の柱が礎石から外れて持ち上がってしまい、
御神酒はみんなひっくり返されて。

　　　　三

音楽学校の窓から
小節やむずかしい音階がきこえてきた
いろんなピアノで、西洋音楽の
音程を練習していたのだ。

A cornet joined them as I waited,
discords struck with every note
promising unstated
concertos, but that bit more remote.

    4

Last night it rained so heavily
the sound was of high winds
clattering leaves.
             Not dogs or cats,
they say it's raining husbands
– as if for these girl graduates
trooping under massed umbrellas
like in Hiroshige, like in Utamaro,
past the stooping gardeners
who, wet leaves hard to brush away,
will doggedly take up birch brooms
and sweep at them tomorrow.

    5

In the garden of the Bard
we found wormwood, wormwood,
a medlar, apricock and may tree.
But where was rue? Where rosemary,
rosemary, that's for remembrance?

ぼくが待っているうち、コルネットの音が加わった、
旋律ごとに打ち鳴らす不協和音は
何かは分からない協奏曲になりそうな予感を
漂わせていたものの、それは遠い先のことになりそうだった。

   四

昨夜はひどい雨だったので
大きな風の音が
葉をばさばさいわせていた。
         「犬猫のよう」に降る雨ではなくて
「亭主のよう」に降る雨なんて表現もあるが、
――これはまるで、この大卒のお嬢さんたちのためにあるような、
広重や歌麿の浮世絵みたいに
たくさんの傘の下に集いつつ
うずくまる園丁たちの傍を通り過ぎる彼女たちのために。
園丁自身、払い去るのが難しい濡れ落ち葉ではあるものの、
不屈の精神で竹ぼうきを手にとって、
明日は本物の濡れ落ち葉を一掃することだろう。

   五

大詩人シェイクスピアの庭で
ぼくらはにがよもぎを見つけた。にがよもぎ、
西洋花梨、アプリコット、それに山査子を。
でも、ヘンルーダはどこかしら？ローズマリーは？
花言葉は「忘れないで」の、ローズマリーはどうしたの？

6

Whether it was orioles
that descant from thick foliage,
or some local souls
at work once more in old age
who whistled on their knees,
I heard survival's celebration
tormenting those with a relation
or two, with whole families
in just twenty seconds gone.

7

We were counting their losses,
their good luck or lack of it
in a wall on the top of a car,
toppled houses and intact ones
side by side in city blocks
like random bombed sites
with phone numbers and names
on signs at the edges of cleared plots
among odd stones and mosses,
minute gardens' flowerpots.

8

The noise of clearing up
came like so many aftershocks;
streets were jammed with dumper trucks,
skips; we kept on hearing

　　　　六

あれは生い茂る葉群らから
美しく歌う高麗ウグイスだったのか、
それとも地元の人が、
老齢ではあるものの再び働き出して、
膝を折りつつ口笛を吹いていたのか、
ぼくは生き残った者たちの喜びが、
親戚縁者の一人や二人、
あるいは一家をまるごと、わずか二十秒が過ぎる間に
喪ってしまった人々を苦しめるのを聞いた。

　　　　七

ぼくらは、人々の損失を数えていた、
人々の幸運を、あるいは不運を数えた、
車の上に落ちてきた壁の一部、
倒壊した家々と無傷の家々が
市街地に隣り合うさま、
それはまるで無差別爆撃地帯のよう、
瓦解して何もなくなった区画の端には
電話番号と名前を書きつけたプラカードがあった、
奇妙なかたちの庭石や、苔や、
盆栽の鉢に紛れながら。

　　　　八

倒壊した街を片づける作業の音が、
たくさんの余震のように響いてくる。
通りは清掃トラックと、運搬用トロッコで
渋滞していた。ぼくらは聞き続けた、

splintered rending cracks
of written-off wood houses
as dainty grabs and bulldozers
moved in on caterpillar tracks.

9

Shaken to its foundations,
the idea of identity's
in mourning for some grounds.
On fields of ashes it dissolves
back fifty years' enduring, a nation's
concrete fissured in these sounds:
'We stopped believing the authorities,
stopped believing in ourselves.'

10

'Real swallows,' you exclaimed
as they nimbly dipped and climbed
over riverbanks, cemented in;
Mount Rokko erased by mist
like apartments swathed with polythene
commanded this crushed area;
another late-flowering cherry
shed its petals under drizzle,
but I missed the araucaria
(that primitive monkey-puzzle tree).

優美なパワーショベルやブルドーザーが
キャタピラの轍にそって動くにつれて、
見限られた木造家屋が
木っ端微塵に倒される音を。

　　　　九

礎石まで揺るがされたのだ、
アイデンティティという考えが、
ある土地に、おのれが寄って立つ土台に、哀悼を捧げる中で。
灰燼と化した野で、五十年の耐久性を持つはずだった
それは溶け去り、国家というコンクリートには、
こうした声の中で亀裂が入った。
「俺らはもうお偉いさんを信じるのをやめた、
自分たちを信じることもやめてしまった」

　　　　十

「本物のつばめよ」ときみは叫んだ
つばめが素早く川面に触れてそれから
セメントで固められた土手を上空へ飛んでいったときに。
霧でよく見えない六甲山は
この壊滅地帯を支配するポリエチレンの
シートでくるまれたマンションのよう。
ありふれた遅咲きの桜が
霧雨のもと、花びらを散らしていたが、
でも、ぼくが懐かしんだのは南洋杉
(あの、原始的な針葉樹だ)。

11

Yellow powder on our noses
was the pollen of camellias:
so perhaps the Muses
are still memory's girls
– as suddenly appears
with a couple of cabbage
whites like flying blossom,
an address book's double page
spread, my last five years'
lives filling them.

12

Beyond the lamp-lit circle
and after dinner talk,
red blazes of azaleas
were breathing in the dark.

As if the lost returned
to make a last goodbye…
They reach us through fresh bushes
shaping up outside.

十一

ぼくらの鼻にくっついた黄色い粉は
椿の花粉だった。
とすると、詩神はやっぱり
記憶の娘たちなのかもしれない
──だって、突如として
空に舞う花びらのような
二匹の紋白蝶とともに
見開きにした二ページ分の住所録が
あらわれて、ぼくの過去五年間の生活が
それを埋めていったのだから。

　　　十二

明かりの灯った円陣と
食後の談話の向こうでは
アザレアの赤い輝きが
暗がりの中で呼吸をしていた。

それはまるで、亡くなった人々が
最後のお別れを告げに戻ってきたかのよう……
死者はぼくらに触れる、戸外で
しゃんと育っている青々とした茂みを通じて。

ITALIAN IN SENDAI

Not long after the rainy season's start
our breakfast-time weather report
predicted a deficiency of sunlight
– as if you needed to be told,
with that patter interrupting grey quiet
and every umbrella unfurled.

Lilting gestures, cadenced words
said what you thought of glass façades,
of buildings clad in toilet-tile,
cheek by jowl with a tin or wood shack
when all your life's been *campanile*,
stucco, responsive plasterwork.

Curtains had opened on another cool spell;
you and I like mercenary soldiers
accumulating reasons to go home
were defenceless against nostalgias
piled with the clouds on some
closed horizon, knowing only too well

that a bottle of wine's not Italy
nor foreigner speaking your language, home,
and the sound made by coffee
bubbling in a machine's upper part
is no better than a short, translated poem –
even if I've learnt it off by heart.

仙台のイタリア人

梅雨に入ったばかりのころ
朝食の時間にやっていた天気予報は
日照時間が不足するだろうと告げた
——まるで、そう教えてもらう必要があったみたいじゃないか、
灰色の静寂を邪魔するようにぱらぱらと降る雨の音や
さまざまな傘の華が咲いているのに加えて。

快活な仕草、抑揚のあることばが
きみがガラスの玄関や、トイレ用のタイルが貼られた
建物について思ったことを述べた。
それはトタンないしは木造の掘っ立て小屋に隣接している。
でも君の生活はこれまでずっと、イタリア風の鐘楼、
化粧漆喰、もっと共鳴力のある石膏細工だったんだ。

いつも通りの寒い日が続く中、カーテンが開けられた。
まるで傭兵みたいに
帰郷の理由を一つ一つ積み重ねるきみとぼくは、
よく見えない地平線上に溜まった
雲のような郷愁に対して、まったく
無防備だったが、それはつくづく思い知っていたからだ

ワインが一瓶あったからってここはイタリアじゃないし、
きみの国の言葉を話す外国人がいたって、自分の家じゃないし、
コーヒー・メイカーの上部で
コーヒーがぽこぽこ音を立てていたとしたって、
そんなもの、短い翻訳詩程度のものに過ぎないことを——
たとえ、ぼくがその詩を暗記していたとしても。

WINTER INTERIORS

for John and Christine Roe

1

Waking to low-angled sunlight
aglow in white curtains, in a sliding screen,
on wooden-framed and sand-encrusted wall,
to the smell of a loaf baked overnight
and, despite the season, kept from harm
in that devastated city of all places,
I lift my good ear from the pillow, turn
(as if no longer needing to yearn
for anything more) and find the warm,
steady-breathing faces
of a mother and child in your chilly room.

2

Though just now, unseasonable snows
like frozen spume on a Hokusai wave
had whitened out the distances,
draped pine branches with their ermine –
though we are not all states, all princes,
and there's never been another School of Love –
back to the days of numbed senses
at condensation-beaded windows
we're doing our best to survive;
though never very good at close family,
at accepting dependence because strong enough,
in the still of a difficult winter, who knows?
Perhaps we'll give it a try.

冬の室内

ジョン・ロウとクリスティーン・ロウにささぐ

　　　　　一

目を覚ましたのは、低く差し込む日の光が
白いカーテンと障子に照り映えて、
木で縁取られた砂壁にも映えて燃えるようだったし、
一晩かけて焼かれたパンの香りがしたからだ。
こんな季節だというのに、パンは傷一つなかった、
全てが灰燼に帰したこの都市にあって。
だから、ぼくはよく聞こえる方の耳を枕から上げ、振り向く
(もうこれ以上、何かに焦がれる必要など
ないという感じで)、そうして見つける、あたたかな、
規則正しい寝息を立て、君たちの冷たい部屋で
眠っている母と子の顔を。

　　　　　二

たった今、季節はずれの雪が
北斎の波の絵にある凍った泡のように、
全てを真っ白にして距離感を消し、
オコジョの毛皮のような雪の垂れ布をまとった松の枝も見えない
　　けれど——
ぼくらは王国でもなければ王侯でもなく、
形而上詩人以来、新たな「愛の学派」は生まれなかったけれど——
水滴でガラスが曇った窓辺での
感覚麻痺の日々に戻り、
それを生き抜くため、ぼくらは全力を尽くしている。
仲の良い家族、なんて決して上手にやれたこともなく、
充分に強いからこそ頼ったり頼られたりを受け入れられる、なんてのも
　　無理だけど、
この難しい冬の静寂の中、誰に分かる?
ぼくら今こそ、試してみようか。

FOR MY DAUGHTER

'We all of us love Miss Matty, and I somehow
think we are all of us better when she is near us.'
Elizabeth Gaskell

This morning at the breakfast table,
what was it about a crow
perched on satellite antennae
above an ice cream tub of snow
caught my daughter's eye?

Below the blackness of that bird,
once more appears our yellow
water tank smeared with rust;
on a white scoop-full's overflow
the same crow comes to rest.

She points, laughs infectiously,
then clutches at her temples;
it seems for my daughter our world's
a mass of picture-book examples,
and we supply the words.

*

This morning at the breakfast table,
they frame a snowy landscape for us:
its quintessence of nothing, a sparrow's
mishap in suburbs, the various
ways of looking at blackbirds or crows …

娘へ

「私たち皆ミス・マティが大好きで、何だか私、私たち皆、
彼女が傍にいると気分が良くなるように感じるの」
エリザベス・ギャスケル

今朝の朝食のテーブルで、
一羽のからすがアイスクリームの
カップみたいな雪の上の
衛星放送のアンテナにとまっている、その
何が一体娘の目をひいたんだろう?

からすの黒さの下にあるのは
またしてもお馴染の、錆で汚れた
黄色い貯水タンク。
ひとさじ分溢れた白い雪の上に
例のからすが一休みに来ているのだ。

彼女はそれを指し、人を釣り込ませるように笑い、
それから自分の両のこめかみを掴む。
どうやら娘にとって、私たちの世界は
無数の絵本の挿絵のようなもので、
それに私たちが詞書きをつけているらしい。

　　　　＊

今朝の朝食のテーブルで
世界という絵本が私たちに見せるのは雪景色
雪の本質は無なんだよ、郊外の
すずめさんには不運だねえ、黒つぐみやからすを見る
にも色んな見方があってね……

Does a bundle of accident and incoherence
alter our morning's breakfast scene?
Or the spirit her laughter brings?
You may well laugh, but laugh again
at these ordinary arrangements of things.

思いがけない出来事や矛盾が重なって
私たちの朝食の風景が変わるのだろうか。
それとも娘が元気いっぱいだから何にでも笑うのか。
きみが笑うのも当然、でも、やっぱり笑い甲斐があるよ、
こういう平凡な出来事にだって。

COAT HANGER

Pegging out shirts on my first-floor balcony,
I happen to notice a white, wire coat hanger
dangling from one low branch of the tree
right by our neighbour's garden.
What's it doing there?

*

Perhaps it's a homage to Jasper Johns
for six months here in the Korean War,
or in memory of the feelings of his friend
who remembered a 'loneliness' from seven years before
'drifting into my ears off Sendai in the snow …'
(but where he saw that whiteness during August '45
I don't for the life of me know).

*

Well, yes, I suppose it could be mine,
blown about by a wind
that unhooks the things you can hang on a line
or bough: an abandoned black plastic umbrella,
the strips of white paper containing bad fortunes,
tied in neat bows, transferred to the tree
– which seems to have absorbed them;
spirited away the luck; at any rate, survived.

*

ハンガー

わが家の二階のベランダでシャツを干していたら
たまたま気付いたのだけれど、白い針金で出来たハンガーが
お隣さんの庭のすぐ傍にある木の下枝で
ぶらぶら揺れている。
奴はあんなところで何をしているのかな。

    *

ひょっとして朝鮮戦争の時代に半年ここにいた
ジャスパー・ジョンズに敬意を表してのことかもしれないし、
あるいは彼の友人の気持ちを偲んでのことかもしれない。
ジョンズを遡ること7年、「雪の仙台沿岸にいる私の耳に忍び寄る」
「さみしさ」を忘れなかった友人を……
(しかし彼が1945年の8月に白銀を見ていたのが一体どこなのか
ぼくにはさっぱり見当も付かないのだけれど)。

    *

ああ、そうだ、もしかしたらあれはぼくの物かも知れない、
風に飛ばされたのかも。
風は、物干し綱や枝に掛けるような物だって
外してしまうから。捨てられた黒いビニール傘や、
几帳面に蝶結びされた運勢の良くない
おみくじなんかが、あの木へと運ばれて
——あの木はそれをみんな吸収してしまったような、
運を全部引き受けてなお、兎も角も生き抜いてきた、そんな風に見える。

    *

Though camouflaged, now
that one more layer of overlapping greens
has painted out winter, some distant love's
skin can still be glimpsed through freckled tones
of bark, sap, chlorophyll; like a phantom limb,
tanned patches come, pale down, a hand –
and so much else that could depend
on a coat hanger among the leaves.

カムフラージュされてしまったけれど——今や
重なり合う緑が一層濃くなって
冬を塗りつぶしてしまったから——遙か遠くの愛しい人の肌がそれでも、
樹皮や、樹液や、葉緑素のまだら模様を通して、
垣間見られる。四肢を失っても人は手足があるかのように感じるもの
　だが、
ぼくにも感じられるんだ。恋人の日灼けしたしみ、薄い産毛、手——
それから、木の間のハンガーにかかっている
他のとてもとてもたくさんのことが。

TYPHOON WEATHER

'Eh' er singt und eh' er aufhört,
Muß der Dichter leben'
Johann Wolfgang Goethe

'If this is life!' you said and sighed,
stumbling over a heap of shoes
one afternoon as we tried to leave,
the children fractious in all that noise.

*

Outside, on a ridge exposed
to every wind that blows,
branches, whole tormented trees
flailed like arms of women
fleeing a rape on some smoky canvas,
like the victim's upraised hands
in Goya's picture of reprisals –
as if the gale could be saying this,
or ripped leaves were expressive of it.

*

Fronds and debris through the air
were damage too; the pummelling rain
in blasts just buffeted our blue car –
while to roll under desperate boughs
struck me as uplift enough
and how it has to be, if this is life.

台風の荒れ模様

「歌う前に、やめる前に、
詩人はまず生きなければならない」
ゲーテ

「これが人生というのなら！」きみはそういってため息をついた、
山と積まれた靴につまずきながら、
ある午後出かけようとした時に――
子供たちも、この風の音でむずかっていた。

   *

外では、あらゆる方面から吹き付ける
風にさらされた山の背で、
枝々が、全身痛めつけられた木々が、
暴行から逃れようともがく女性の腕のように、
くすぶったキャンバスの上で振り動いている。
ゴヤの報復的拿捕の絵にある
被害者が両手を上げたところみたいだろう――
まるで、大風がこんなことを語り得るみたいな、
ちぎれた葉っぱがそれを表現し得るかのような。

   *

空中を舞っている椰子の葉や、何かの破片も
損害だ。したたかに降る雨が
突風の中、ぼくらの青い車にひたすら打ち付け――
やけくそみたいな大枝の下、車を転がす間に
ぼくは突然思った、これも十分人を高揚させるし
かくあるべきなんだろう、これが人生というのなら。

ANIMAL SENDAI

'What was it he did a tail
at all on Animal Sendai?'
James Joyce

On a normal Sunday inside the zoo's
fenced precincts families traipse
over crazed asphalt, collapsed curbs
down what seem suburbs' avenues;
have themselves snapped near brute
beasts, dumb animals, creatures
of our curiosity in cages, pens,
or smiling from behind the bars
of an unlocked cell marked: *homo sapiens* –
but only for a moment; there they are
a bit like Parma wallabies,
surviving though their seasons
come upside down, a polar bear
who just copes with the climate
and big cats basking in a winter sun's
fitful warmth; far shrieks, far cries –
I'm putting in a word for them.

I'm putting in a word
for glimpses of Miyagi bay's
swerving shore grown visible
through clearer air, the wind chill
round picnic spots and angled boughs
of cherry, plum, the cedar, pine;
for grass blades that two elephants uproot
or take out of each other's mouths;
a word for those crazed monkeys,
their sorrowful noises overhead;

アニマル・センダイ

「彼がし尾ったあれは何だ
アニマル・センダイの祝日に」
ジェイムズ・ジョイス

なんでもない日曜日、フェンスで仕切られた
動物園の構内で家族連れがうろうろしている。
ひびの入ったアスファルトの上を、崩れた
郊外の並木道みたいなところへ続く曲がり角を。
彼らは、猛獣や口のきけない動物や
ぼくらの好奇心のためにかごや檻に入れられた
生き物のそばで指を鳴らしたり、
「ホモ・サピエンス」と記された、鍵のかかっていない房に
ついた手すりの向こう側で微笑んだりしている——
でも、それも束の間のこと。人間はそこで、
まったく逆さまの季節を耐え抜く
パルマ・ワラビーや、ここの気候を
なんとか生き延びているにすぎない北極グマや
冬の太陽の断続的な暖かさの中ひなたぼっこする
ネコ科の猛獣にちょっと似ている。遠い鳴き声、遠い叫び——
ぼくはそれに、ことばを当てている。

そう、ぼくはことばを当てているんだ、
ところどころ垣間見える仙台湾の
曲がりくねった浜辺が、いつもより澄んだ空気の中
やがて見えなくなっていくさまに、ピクニック用地や
桜、梅、杉、松の木々の斜めに伸びた
枝を取り巻く風の冷たさに。
二匹の象が根こぎにしたり、
お互いの口から取り出しあっている草の葉にも。
狂ったように騒ぐあの猿たちにも、ことばを当てよう。
猿聲天上に哀し、と。

for flakes of gravel, a mandril's gaze,
dog fox's stink; for the laughing hyena
in yet another humdrum dusk
where a smith's gazelle with broken horn
screams out against the isolation –
and by this prison house of their days,
its shabbiness, I'm putting in a
word for these things mute.

砂利の薄片に、マンドリルの眼差しに、
それから雄ギツネの臭気にも。いつも通りの平凡な黄昏のなか
笑っているかのような顔したハイエナにも、ことばを当てよう。
そこでは、角の折れたスミスかもしかが一頭、
孤独と戦いながら叫びをあげている——
彼らが日々を過ごすその牢獄のそば、
そのみすぼらしさの傍らで、ぼくはことばを当てる
これらもの言わぬものたちに代わって。

WINTER ZOO ENCOUNTER

> 'You know what I was,
> You see what I am: change me, change me!'
> Randall Jarrell

The woman at the Yagiyama Zoo
approached us when she heard
her language being spoken.
The children wouldn't understand
if she used her mother tongue.
I couldn't tell where she was from,
surrounded by her local family
living in some nearby town.
The woman at the Yagiyama Zoo
had been away too long.

Another Florentine in exile
she unburdened her life story,
told us how she met her husband,
how he brought her home;
but because they did not hope
to return for years on end
there were pauses, occasional slips
of grammar as she rummaged
the vulgar tongue for idiom,
a telling phrase or word.

Like birds that know their limit,
won't fly against the mesh
curving over each plumed head,
she seemed remote, reflected
'In the eyes of animals ... trapped
As I am trapped', a phrase

冬の動物園での邂逅

　　　　　　　「かつての私を先刻ご承知で
今の私もお見通しでしょ。私を変えて、変えてよ!」
　　ランドル・ジャレル

八木山動物園で出逢った女性、
自分のお国言葉が話されるのを
耳にして、ぼくたちに近寄ってきた、
実の子でも分からないだろう
お母さんが母語を使ったりしたら。
ぼくには、彼女の出身地が分からなかった、
近くの町に住んでいるという
婚家の家族に囲まれているものだから。
八木山動物園の女、
あまりに長いことお国を離れてしまったのだ。

異郷生活のフィレンツェ人がここにも一人、
彼女は自分のライフ・ストーリーを打ち明けて、
ぼくたちに教えてくれた。夫とどんな風に出逢い、
彼がどんな風に妻を連れ帰ったかを。
けれど、二人は何年もずっと
帰ることは望まぬ気持ちだったからと
言葉に詰まることや、文法の間違いもあった、
彼女が、俗語から
ぴったりの言い回しを、効果的な語句、
そのものずばりの一言を探すときには。

自分たちの境界を知っていて、
冠毛の上でゆるやかなカーブを描く
網の向こうへは飛ぼうとはしない鳥のように、
彼女は遠くに見えた、反射しているようだった
「動物たちの目の中に……囚われの身
私が囚われているのと同じ」——この言葉は

that came to mind here in the cold.
Rare birds flapped from a twisted bough
to the guano-covered ground
inside this form of air.

Of all the exogamous marriages
changing us, I thought of ours –
how a love drew me towards
but withdrew her from those words,
words we use now to describe
beaver couples gnawing their bars
as Suffolk sheep lyrically bleat
and the woman at the Yagiyama Zoo
spoke not wanting to forget
the dialect of her tribe.

寒さのなか、そこでふと思い浮かんだもの。
珍しい鳥たちが、ねじれたとまり木から
糞が分厚く堆積した地面へと移動していた、
区切られた型枠の空気のなかで。

人々を変えてしまうあらゆる異種族婚
のなかでも、ぼくはぼくと妻の結婚を考えた——
一つの愛がいかにあの言葉にぼくを引きつけつつ
彼女のことは遠ざけてしまったか、
棒杭をかじるビーバーの夫婦を
語るのにぼくらが今使っている言葉、
その間もサフォーク産の羊は抒情的にいななき、
八木山動物園の女は喋り続けた
自分の種族の土地言葉を
忘れたくなくて。

EQUIVOCAL ISLE

'Die Liebe hat einen Triumph und der Tod hat einen ...'
Ingeborg Bachmann

From out the shallows, our small craft,
its motor idling under cliffs'
wave-cut sandstone hieroglyphics,
expertly is left to drift.

By way of a narrow, rocky strait
with pine tree roots like varicose veins
and natural bonsai on each ledge
(our hull fitted tightly through it)
we enter almost open sea.

Up ahead, as fresh wind lifts,
an island on the skyline,
an island bearded with pine tree tufts
echoes the dark in its design.

A few outlying rocks stand guard.
The salt-white lighthouse at its point
conjures an offing, ambivalent
urges to approach or veer shoreward
in brightness on the water.

Seagulls take snacks from outstretched hands;
they hang above the stern and cry.

Love triumphs over nobody
and, for that matter, neither does death –
its cypress isle, stark temple, calm
sea, pale-shrouded soul: its kitsch.

あいまいな島

「愛は勝利をおさめ、死もまた……」
インゲボルグ・バッハマン

浅瀬から出たぼくらの小さな船は、
そのモーターの空転は、波に削られて
象形文字のようになっている岸壁の下、
熟練の技で浮くがまま。

細い、岩のごつごつした海峡を通り過ぎれば、
そこには静脈瘤のように膨れた根を見せる松
そして左右の岩礁にはまるで天然の盆栽
(ぼくらの船は岩礁すれすれに進む)
そして、ほとんど外海に近いところまで行く。

爽やかな風が強まるなか、前方を見やれば、
水平線に島が一つ、
松葉の房で髭を生やしたみたいな島は
意匠として闇を思わせる。

遠くに見える岩々が護衛をしている。
塩のように白い灯台はその点で
沖合を、曖昧な衝動を呼び起こす
——近づきたいような、岸へ引き返したいような——
水面の輝きの中。

鴎は乗船客がうんと伸ばした手からスナックをもらう。
鴎は船尾をいつまでも飛び回り、鳴く。

愛は誰に勝利をおさめることもない、
それに、言わせてもらえば、死だってそうなのだ。
死がつかさどる糸杉の島、がらんとしたお寺、凪いだ海、
青白い経帷子を纏った魂も。死のキッチュさも。

Death triumphs over nobody.

Off in the lanes ships roll and pitch.
The craft's outboard accelerates
on stiffening swell where seagulls skrike,
that equivocal island's silhouette
diminishing in our wake.

死は誰にも勝利したりしない。

沖合の航路では、船は縦に揺れ横に揺れる。
我らの船の船外モーターが、鴎が甲高くわめく中
強くうねる大波に加速すると、
あのあいまいな島のシルエットは
我らの船の航跡のうちに消えてゆく。

ALL AROUND

1

On this bright-cold day in autumn
low sun paints its chiaroscuro
all around us: like a chessboard,
shadow and the gleaming air
are set as lines, as ways of moving;
paths paved with crisp detritus
have their signposts, corner mirrors,
where, routinely pacing on,
I lose the sense of being aimed –
of being governed by direction.

2

In gorges where sun doesn't reach
or the pine groves' sudden coolness,
we're surrounded by this life.

And autumn pays us back in kind –
as if, as if the thought of death
lent it your vitality.

3

Now too many leaves have fallen.
Summer not even a memory,
let alone a theme to live by,
early autumns in Japan
come floating from a cloudless sky.

辺り一面に

　　　　一

この冴え冴えと晴れた秋の日に
低い太陽が辺り一面をみな明暗対照法で
塗っている。チェス盤のように、
影とちらちら光る大気とが
動き方を示す動線になっている。
アスファルトのあちこちにひびの入った小径には
標識あり、カーブミラーあり、
毎日のように歩いているこの道では
ぼくは何者かに意図された存在という感じが——
何らかの方向付けをされている感じがしない。

　　　　二

日の光も届かない渓谷で、また
松林に入って突然空気が涼しくなるようなとき、
ぼくらはこの生に取り巻かれている。

すると秋はぼくらに同じ物をお返ししてくれる——
まるで、まるで、死について思いめぐらすと
君の生命力を秋に与えてしまうかのよう。

　　　　三

今や、葉もあんまりたくさん落ちてしまった。
夏の思い出なんて、ひとかけらもないし、
まして、夏が生きる指針に成り得るはずもない。
日本の初秋はいつも
雲一つない空からぷかりと浮かんでやって来る。

Red maple hanging on stripped branches
till the very last breath takes them,
all around, are ghastly emblems;
I'm obsessed with you, this autumn,
pricing yourself up out of life.

    4

But that's as maybe, you not here;
whereas we, the living, want
to know why hawks, why gusted leaves,
why stones and skies were not enough?

The child in arms, child left to cry,
a season loved more than the others,
hints of winter, earthly hush,
why were none of these enough?

    5

All around, dark earthworks rise;
sun's angle keeps the shadows long.

On every side, hortensias'
bluish globes are still intact,

the ginkgo leaves, a lemon yellow,
tousled by that passing bus.

This chilly sunlight: death or love,
how they wax and wane in us!

紅葉した楓の葉が、葉の落ちた枝にぶらりと下がっている。
生命の最後の一吹きが彼らを連れ去ってしまうまで。
辺り一面が、ぞっとするような寓意画だ。
この秋、ぼくは君に取り憑かれている、
貴すぎて、生者の世界にいられなくなった君に。

　　　四

でもそれも場違いかも知れない、君がここにいない以上。
それでもぼくらは、生きている者たちは、知りたいのだ、
どうして鷹では、どうして吹き散らされた葉では、
どうして石や空では、十分ではなかったのだろう？

腕の中の子供、泣くがままに放っておかれた子供、
どの季節よりも愛された季節、
冬の到来をほのめかすもの、大地の静けさ、
どうしてこれらの何一つとして、十分ではなかったのだろう？

　　　五

辺り一面に、黒ずんだ土塊が盛り上がっている。
太陽の角度で、影が長く伸びる。

どちらを向いても、紫陽花の
青みがかった丸い花がまだ綺麗なままだ。

檸檬色した銀杏の葉は
通り過ぎるバスのせいでくちゃくちゃだ。

この冴え冴えとした日の光。死なのか、愛なのか、
この二つは何とまあ私たちの中で満ちては欠けてゆくのだろう！

OCCASIONAL SUNSET

Closing curtains on an opened-up sky
you pause to let change happen
in its own time or while
crows wheel about like bits of night
the turquoise vault's empurpled,
pink-flecked, become lurid violet.

Lower, leaf cluster and grass pile
turn viridian from emerald
in the falling night which follows
like a threat or a cadence
swelling time gone as work-filled blurs
now to a green after-light.

So even the worst days were ended
leaving us to figure out the dark –
how it's not what anybody intended,
but this come by default that says
we were alive to our lives
when it was one of those days.

たまたまの日没

ひらけた空にカーテンを引こうとして
君はふと手を止め、変化が向こうのタイミングで
起こるに任せるとその間にも
からすが夜のかけらみたいに辺りを旋回するうちに
ターコイズ・ブルーの大空が紫色になり、
ピンク色が混じってきて、どぎつい青紫になる。

その下では、葉群らと刈草の山が
夜のとばりが降りるにつれて、エメラルド色から
青緑に変わるが、夜が日没を追いかけるのはまるで
何かの脅しかそれとも韻律のように
過ぎ去った時間を膨らませるが、その間にも仕事ばかりでぼんやりした
　一日が
今や緑色の残照に変わってゆく。

こんな風に最悪の日々だって終わりを告げたのだ、
ぼくたちに闇というものを理解させて去っていったのだ——
そんなこと誰だって好きこのんでやることではなく、
いわばこちらの手の出せないうちに勝手に来たこと、それが教えてくれる
　のは
ぼくらは自分の人生の一瞬一瞬を生きたということ、
最悪の日々に。

PASTA-MAKING

How like the forearm of that laundress
pressing her iron in a picture by Degas
comes your arm as you help dough through
a pasta machine, how like you
to be making things happen as if chance
mixtures of ingredients this once
were a recipe for happiness
kneaded, rolled with a pin and, yes,
how like you, how like the flame-flowered apron
set off by white blouse folds to be just one
of the details held for their own sake –
like that spray of arranged daisy petals or like
the plain wood board with dusting of flour,
or your torso leant forward lending more power
to bare elbows, more force to your forearms –
and these not random items
composing the moment's promise –
yes, how like you this
open window's lifting pines
with the stuck groove of a stray cat's whines
how like a child's half-consoled crying,
its echo taken up in blue fathomless sky …

パスタ作り

なんとまあドガの絵に出てくる
アイロンがけをする洗濯女の前腕が
パスタの製麺機に生地を入れている君の腕と
重なるんだよ、なんとまあ
何かをしようとしている君がまるで
今回だけ巧まずして混ざり合った原料を
こねたり綿棒で伸ばしたりした
幸福のレシピみたいなんだ、そう、
なんとまあ君が、なんとまあ、白いブラウスの皺と好対照の
君の橙色の花模様のエプロンが、ただそれ自身の
美しさのために心に留め置かれる日常の小さなことのよう——
きれいに並んだ雛菊の花びら模様や
打ち粉をふったまな板に、
むき出しの肘にもっと力を込めようと、前腕に
もっと力を入れようと前屈みになっている君の上半身なんかが——
そしてこれらのでたらめでない一つ一つのことが
束の間の安心感を与えてくれるんだ——
そうだ、なんてまあ君はこの
開いた窓に高く揺れる松の木のようだろう
そこでは迷い猫のか細い鳴き声が壊れたレコードみたいに続く
なんてまあ機嫌が直りかけの赤ちゃんの泣き声に似ていることだろう、
そのこだまが果てしない青空に響いてゆくよ……

ALIEN REGISTRATION

'Dr Robinson, you need to renew
your alienation card ...'

Daybreak and even the clouds flake
away at their edges like fish scales,
like rust, like blood on your lenses.
For a moment, I'm really not sure
where this particular darkness visible
might be, and you know how it is, an obscure
remorse or worse, something worse
sticks round the memories of words;
and I squirm as between clock and bed,
porous with daylight, darker shapes
fill out the outline in a vanity mirror
speckled at its edges; and sure enough,
glancing at the photograph,
you notice a face they no longer recognize.

So you know, you don't need to be told
how the frustrations will gather
at a stuck traffic signal or stop-sign,
when queues in official places
leave us all at the end of our tether ...
There'll be little else for it but to take
that gap between sky and unfenced concrete
as storm clouds come sloping above us
to shed their droplets on the finest grey
dust you might ever hate to see –
being humbled by that disintegrating day
when any slight change in the weather
was enough to be wondering what in the world
could possibly put it back together?

外国人登録
<small>エイリアン・レジストレーション</small>

「ロビンソン先生、先生の
<small>エイリアネーション</small>
疎　外　感カードを更新しなくては……」

夜が明けると、ちぎれ雲までが
——その端の方は魚の鱗みたいになっているのだけれど——
サビのように、水晶体の充血のように赤くなる。
束の間、ぼくは、この〈目に見えるほどの闇〉が
ある場所がよく分からず、すると分かってもらえるだろうが、
あいまいな悔恨とか、それよりひどい、何かそれよりひどいものが
ことばの記憶の周囲にくっついてくる。
そしてぼくはのたくるが、その間にも、目覚まし時計とベッドに挟まれ
太陽の光で穴だらけにされた暗いものの形が、
縁がまだら模様の化粧鏡の中ではっきりとした輪郭を
取り始める。すると間違いないことだが、
写真をちらりと眺めやれば、
彼らにはとても識別できない顔を認めるのだ。

だから分かるだろう、言われるまでもない、
「この先行き止まり」や「一時停止」の標識で
欲求不満がどんなにたまってしまうことか、
お役所の行列がぼくらみんなを
いつもの列の端っこに置いてけぼりにするようなときには……
そこでは、やれることはもう何もない、隙をついて
空と塀のないコンクリートの間を出し抜いてやるほか。
今しも嵐を予感させる雲がゆっくりと頭上に垂れ込め
全く見るのも嫌になるほど微小な
灰色のちりの上に、小さな滴を落とすところだが——
要するに、このバラバラになってしまいそうな一日に凹まされていたのだ
天気がほんのちょっと変わっただけでも、一体今日という日を
立て直してくれるものは有り得るのかと訝しむほどの。

CALM AUTUMN

'Stretched out on the floor,
ear to a short-wave radio,
we were bent to hear
would it be peace or war?'

After the traumas, storms and disappointments
sometimes an autumnal calm
day, like this one, comes as if in recompense;
yes and at moments like this one,
lucky, it's all I can do to enjoy
a strobe-effect of sunlight through the high,
anti-suicide fence's bars
as I take the same old bridge across that gorge.

There's a lurid yellow glow above the sea;
there are stark factory
smoke-stacks standing out against it.
Then flashed off the estuary
are similar tints like a boy with a mirror, sky
still showing its complement of hawks,
and again that interrupted sun
signals like an echo of the ships within far gulfs.

*

You see the line of national flags
at a sports day's end when somebody drags it
through grey dust. I'm put out by swags
strung across roof-space in a gym –
then think again now rows of them

静かな秋

「床に寝転がり、
短波のラジオに
ぼくらは熱心に耳を傾けた
どうなるのだ、戦争か平和か」

トラウマを経験して、嵐のような日々を送り、失望したりした後に
時々、今日のように
秋の静かな日が、償いのようにやってくることがある。
そう、時には今日みたいな日が。
運がいい、これがぼくのできる精一杯だ
ストロボ効果のかかった太陽光が、自殺防止用の
高壁の柵越しに射し込むのを楽しむことが、
峡谷に掛かったいつものあの橋を渡る際に。

海の上にはぞっとするような黄色が輝いている。
やけに目立つ工場の
煙突の煙が何本も、海に対して屹立している。
入り江の向こうでちらちらするのは
鏡を持った少年を思わせる色の光の反射、空は
なお空間を補う鷹の姿を見せている、
それからさきほど翳った日がまた
ぱっと合図を送るのが、まるで遠くの湾にいる船のこだまのようだ。

　　　　　*

国旗が一列に並んでいるのが見えるだろう、
体育の日の終わり、誰かが灰色の風塵の中
それを引きずって、
　　　　　　　そしてぼくは体育館の
天井に張り巡らされた花綱に辟易気味——
そしてまた思い出す、それらが何本も

hang limp above the Luna-Park
in a post-dusk, a first dark.

      *

And yet once more I'm dealing
with the thought of us stretched out on a mat floor
in another seaport, feeling
nausea come like the breakers at its groyne –
heard too in our shore hotel;
ear to a short-wave radio,
through the crackle of static we were trying to tell
would it be peace or war …

      *

It would be war; but now these twelve years later
we see-saw in a rhythm with the days
while leaves are cascading from branches in utter
confusion, strewn over avenues and drives,
are clawed at like the last rags on frayed trees;
and, as when a cartoon character
steps inadvertently out above a drop,
from nowhere somebody among us says:

Don't look, but we're having the time of our lives.

ルナ・パーク遊園地の上にだらりと垂れ下がっているのを、
日が沈んだばかりの、最初の闇が訪れる頃に。

　　　　＊

それでもまたぼくは、畳の上に
みんなで寝転がっていたあの頃の気持ちと向き合っている、
別の港町で、吐き気が
防波堤にうち寄せる波浪のように襲ってくるのを感じながら——
浜辺の宿にも、それは聞こえてきた。
短波のラジオに耳を傾け、
パチパチと聞こえる雑音の中、ぼくらは
戦争か平和かを、知ろうとしていた……

　　　　＊

どうやら戦争になりそうだ。しかし今や十二年が経過して、ぼくらが
シーソーのように、日々のリズムに乗って一進一退を繰り返して
　　いる間
葉っぱは枝からさらさら落ちているけれど、それは完全な
混乱状態で、街路や車道に散らばって、
ぼろぼろになった木々の最後の断片のように掻き集められる。
そして、漫画のキャラクターが不用意に
足を踏み外して急降下する時のような気持ちになると、
何処からともなく身内の誰かが言う——

「考えちゃだめよ、せっかくいい時なんだから」

WHAT HAVE YOU

for Adrian and Margaret

And even if it was the Greek word
you saw, what equally caught your eye
as we paused by a small tomb yard,
each stone with its proffered pot or cup,
was a flapping red-black butterfly
stuck perhaps on the open lip
of a silvered can of Asahi Dry …
Yes, that's what struck your eye.

君が見たものは

エイドリアンとマーガレットにささぐ

すると、たとえ君が墓石に刻まれたギリシャ語に
目を留めたにせよ、同様に君の目をとらえたのは、
ぼくらが傍らで立ち止まった小さな霊園の
墓石の一つ一つに花瓶やお酒のコップがお供えしてあるところに
赤と黒の蝶がひらひら飛んでいる姿で
しかもその蝶が、ひょっとして「アサヒ・ドライ」の銀色をした缶の
飲み口に刺さっていたんだということなのか……
なるほど、君の目を釘付けにしたものはそれか。

FROM THE WORLD

'… unconditions himself
from those circumstances …'

    1

Now, their mothballed power station
underneath a cloudy sky,
it doesn't have that much to say
for itself in a glitter-less autumn light –
its wharves abandoned, still and tidy
cranes, oil storage, not a trace
of smoke from three red-and-white-striped chimneys
overlooking pine-topped islands in the bay.

    2

I'm staring out towards those islands
on a near horizon,
taking in their power station
as one who has mislaid the plot
or storyline, so it can tell
itself without me, as one who's forgot
and gone and left felt phrases
into which we disappear …
I'm staring out towards those islands.

    3

Though wanting a story to carry us over
every twist and turn
in fates that wound you up here,
here I've wound up, nonetheless.

この世界より

「……そういう状況から
あえて自分の条件を外すのだ……」

　　　　一

おや、防虫剤みたいな発電所が
曇り空の下に見えるが
それ自体は取り立てて何というほどのこともない
ぎらつきのない秋の光の中では──
打ち棄てられた埠頭、静かで整然とした
クレーン、石油倉庫、紅白の縞を
成す三本の煙突からは一条の煙もなく
ただ入江の松の小島を見下ろすばかり。

　　　　二

ぼくは見つめる、これらの島々が
水平線近くに浮かぶ方を。
発電所を受け入れるには、
自分のことを、粗筋や構想をうっかり忘れた
誰かさんと見なせばいい、そうすれば奴もおのずと
ぼく無しでやっていけるはず、奴は忘れて行ってしまって
心にしみた言葉だけを後に残した誰かさん、
そういう言葉の中へぼくらは消えていく……
ぼくは相変わらず島々の方を見つめている。

　　　　三

君をここに行き着かせた運命の
あらゆる有為転変をぼくらが
くぐり抜けて行くための物語が欲しいと思いつつも、
結局ぼくもここに行き着いた、というわけ。

You see me in vacant or in pensive mood
and it's as if I'd lost it,
lost the thread of one
staring towards those pine-topped islands'
sights for sore eyes, or that eyesore
of a moth-balled power station.

    4

But still glimpsed pine cones, tombs, wave-curved
declivities and yacht-hull shapes
add up to a drawn-out meaning
when carved birds peck at wooden grapes,
blue crows had cleared their throats this morning
and in a daze I might discover
how, pressures past, it points towards
possibilities in other words.

    5

You see blue or white rags flap at poles;
they outline oyster farms and if not
tales themselves stand in for one –
which might as well be about that moth-balled power station
setting off the beauty of their beauty spot.

君は、ぼくがぼんやりして物思わしげなのを見て取る。
それはまるでぼくが物語を失くしたみたいな、
凧の糸が切れてしまったような、
障りのある目に優しい、美しい松の島々の方を
あるいは目障りな、醜い防虫剤の発電所の方を
見つめている人とつながれずに。

　　　四

それでも今なお、松ぼっくり、墓石、波型の
下り坂にヨットの船体なぞがちらちら見えると
それが積み重なって意味が引き出される、
彫刻の鳥が木製のぶどうをついばむと。
そういえば、青がらすが今朝かあかあと咳払いしていたっけ、
このぼんやりした中で、悟れるかも知れない、
プレッシャーが過ぎ去れば、
他の言葉への可能性も指し示されるのではないか。

　　　五

竿に青や白の旗が結ばれてるのが見えるだろう。
牡蠣の養殖場の境界線を示すんだ、もし違っていても
おのずと別の物語が代わりを務めてくれるさ——
代役の物語がたとえ防虫剤の発電所だって、悪くない
つけボクロのように景勝地の美しさを引き立たせているんだから。

LAST RESORT

For the ones who go and those about to stay,
two autumns: they're turning decay
in another of the spa towns money forgot
to contradictory signs and tokens –
like ripened apples or purple potatoes,
dropped leaves borne down-river, for ever
alighting to drift where the ducks sun themselves.
And I gaze at deserted bed- and bath-rooms
of bankrupted hotels ...
Their proprietors had nothing else to do but walk away.

Where, once upon a time, there were stories to tell
now it's all maybe, maybe and perhaps
for ones bitten by mosquitoes
at a terraced vantage point
with smoke columns rising from rice-field fires,
the ones who must endure this season's
boredoms, its nervous collapse;
they're fretful about what, not leaving, they'll miss
and grieve for younger selves, ones
long-squandered on a promise,
and gaze at those hotels like scuttled battleships.

最後の頼りの保養地

去りゆく人のため、留まる人のため、
秋には二種類ある。ここの人たちは落魄して、
——お金に見捨てられた数多の温泉街の一つに居るから——
互いに矛盾するしるしや象徴になりつつある。
それはまるで、熟れたりんごや紫芋、
下流へと運ばれてゆく落ち葉なんかが、常に
川面に落ちては、あひるが日向ぼっこをしている辺りに流れてくるような
　もの。
そしてぼくは、つぶれた旅館の今はもう使われていない
客室や浴室を眺める……
所有者は、立ち去り行くよりほか手の打ちようがなかったのだ。

そこでも昔は、語るべき物語があったのだ
今では、全てが「ひょっとして」、「あるいは」、「もしも」の話しかなく、
それも展望テラスで
蚊に食われた人のため、
——そこからは田んぼに放った火から立ち上る細い煙が見える——
この季節の退屈と、神経に堪える荒廃ぶりを
耐え抜かねばならない人のため。
彼らは、自分が立ち去るわけでもないのに失ってしまうものを思って苛々し
若かりし頃の自分を思っては嘆く。約束をあてにして
長いこと無駄をしてしまったひとたちなのだ。
そして彼らは、沈没した軍艦のような旅館の群れを見つめる。

SILENCE REVISTED

'What silence
penetrating rock
the voice of the cicada'
Matsuo Bashō

After the gauntlet of parking attendants,
present vendors, signs
any tourist trap wants,
one early May we were making that climb
again up a cliff-front
with pauses and vertigo
at breath-taking stone steps, outcrops, viewing platforms
precarious on narrow, high ledges.

From here I look down to the hills'
profiles in a haze;
for, yes, there was mist across valleys this time
all seen without alien
sensations of years ago,
with no ten years' bickering, sulks or resentments,
tit-for-tats, cries …
In the silence, I was wondering where they had gone.

Here again, the eyes have it; they're ravished
by ivy inching on a wall,
the azaleas' moment under bruised skies,
and because by temple plots
I was tempted still to pick a quarrel
but thought better of it,
(as if sounds had all been absorbed into rock)
it seemed that what the landscape wanted
was only for us to rise above it.

再訪の閑さや

「閑さや
岩にしみいる
蝉の声」
松尾芭蕉

両側に立ち並ぶ駐車場係員、
土産物売り、その他、観光客を惑わす
あらゆる兆候に挟まれ、それを何かの罰みたいに通り過ぎ、
五月初めのある日、ぼくたちは山を登っていた。
再びあの断崖絶壁に向かって
時に立ち止まり、時に目眩を感じた。
息を飲むような石段に、露出した岩石に、狭く高い岩棚の
上に危なっかしく作られた展望台に。

ここからぼくは見下ろす、
もやの中に浮かぶ山々の稜線を。
というのも、そう、今回は谷に霧がかかっていて
全てのものが何年も昔に来たときとは違って見えたのだ、
全く異質なものを見たときのあの衝撃はなくなっていたのだ。
十年に渡る諍い、不機嫌、あるいは憤慨もなく、
売り言葉に買い言葉、泣き声もなく……
静寂の中、ぼくはそれらが何処へ行ってしまったのだろうと考えていた。

ここでまた、この 目（アイズ） が捉えるのは 是（アイズ） が勝る光景。惹きつけられたのだ、
壁に沿ってゆっくり広がってゆく蔦に、
霧の垂れ込めた空の下、咲き誇るアザレアに、
そしてぼくは寺の境内にいて
また喧嘩でも始めたいような誘惑に駆られたのだけれど
そこは考え直したものだから、
（まるで喧騒がみな、岩にしみいってしまったよう）
この景色が望んでいるのはただ一つ、
ぼくらが問題を乗り越えることのように見えた。

行く我に
とゞまる汝に
秋二つ

正岡子規

For me, who must go,
and you remaining behind
two different autumns

Masaoka Shiki

ALL TIMES ARE LOCAL

for Giulia

1

Undaunting, your thousand-piece jigsaw
shows a projection of the whole wide world
and, done, it lies still on that table
like a reconstruction,
a reconstruction of our moments
separated by left times and spaces
put together here.

2

Although not far from Greenwich now
or Brunel's brick-arched bridge,
this gazing through your bedroom window
brings them back to mind –
the dusks on near or gone horizons
and his first Great Western
instituting railway-time.

3

So it's about your own time too
and family resemblances
shifted by walls of chronometer dials,
each one dependent on further place-names
through transit lounge to boarding gate;
you've reassembled all of that
imagining returns to Sendai,
your nostalgia for Japan.

あらゆる時間は現地時間

ジュリアへ

　　　　一

恐ろしくはない、君の1000ピースのジグソー・パズルは
この広い全世界を示す地図で、
いったん完成したら、いつまでもテーブルの上にあって
何かの再建工事のよう。
ぼくらの一瞬一瞬が、再建されているのだ、
過ぎ去りし時間と空間によって隔てられた瞬間が
ここに集められている。

　　　　二

グリニッジからそう遠くないところに住んでいて、
ブルネルの赤煉瓦のアーチ型鉄橋も近いのだけれど、
君の部屋の窓からこんな風に外をじっと見ると、
心に蘇るのは——
最近の、あるいは遠い昔の地平線にかかる夕闇と
彼のファースト・グレイト・ウェスタン鉄道が制定した
列車の時間。

　　　　三

だからこれは君自身の時間についての話でもあり、
家族的類似が、
クロノメーターの時計盤がたくさん掛かった壁で移り変わってきた話
　　でもあり、
そのそれぞれが、さらに先の地名を当てにして
乗り継ぎ便のロビーや搭乗口を通り過ぎてゆくのだ。
君はそれらを全て拾い集めて組み立てた、
仙台への里帰りを想像しながら、
つまり日本への郷愁に浸りながら。

4

Love moves the attentive hand, the eye,
to recollect arranging shadows
long before railway- or clock-time;
it interlocks pieces, shows
through flickers from a scented candle flame
everything everywhere equally here
in world present tenses.

四

注意深い手と、目を、動かすのは愛
列車時間や時計時間より遥かに昔から存在する
影のような遠い思い出の配置を思い出すため。
愛が各ピースを結合させ、
香りつきキャンドルの炎のゆらめきを通して
見せてくれるのだ。あらゆる場所に等しく存在する全てのものを、
世界中に染み渡る〈今〉という時間の中で。

www.ingramcontent.com/pod-product-compliance
Lightning Source LLC
Chambersburg PA
CBHW020916090426
42736CB00008B/662